OECD/G20 Base Erosion and Profit Shifting Project

Making Dispute Resolution Mechanisms More Effective, Action 14 - 2015 Final Report

This document and any map included herein are without prejudice to the status of or sovereignty over any territory, to the delimitation of international frontiers and boundaries and to the name of any territory, city or area.

Please cite this publication as:
OECD (2015), *Making Dispute Resolution Mechanisms More Effective, Action 14 - 2015 Final Report*, OECD/G20 Base Erosion and Profit Shifting Project, OECD Publishing, Paris.
http://dx.doi.org/10.1787/9789264241633-en

ISBN 978-92-64-24158-9 (print)
ISBN 978-92-64-24163-3 (PDF)

Series: OECD/G20 Base Erosion and Profit Shifting Project
ISSN 2313-2604 (print)
ISSN 2313-2612 (online)

Photo credits: Cover © ninog – Fotolia.com

Corrigenda to OECD publications may be found on line at: *www.oecd.org/about/publishing/corrigenda.htm*.

Foreword

International tax issues have never been as high on the political agenda as they are today. The integration of national economies and markets has increased substantially in recent years, putting a strain on the international tax rules, which were designed more than a century ago. Weaknesses in the current rules create opportunities for base erosion and profit shifting (BEPS), requiring bold moves by policy makers to restore confidence in the system and ensure that profits are taxed where economic activities take place and value is created.

Following the release of the report *Addressing Base Erosion and Profit Shifting* in February 2013, OECD and G20 countries adopted a 15-point Action Plan to address BEPS in September 2013. The Action Plan identified 15 actions along three key pillars: introducing coherence in the domestic rules that affect cross-border activities, reinforcing substance requirements in the existing international standards, and improving transparency as well as certainty.

Since then, all G20 and OECD countries have worked on an equal footing and the European Commission also provided its views throughout the BEPS project. Developing countries have been engaged extensively via a number of different mechanisms, including direct participation in the Committee on Fiscal Affairs. In addition, regional tax organisations such as the African Tax Administration Forum, the *Centre de rencontre des administrations fiscales* and the *Centro Interamericano de Administraciones Tributarias*, joined international organisations such as the International Monetary Fund, the World Bank and the United Nations, in contributing to the work. Stakeholders have been consulted at length: in total, the BEPS project received more than 1 400 submissions from industry, advisers, NGOs and academics. Fourteen public consultations were held, streamed live on line, as were webcasts where the OECD Secretariat periodically updated the public and answered questions.

After two years of work, the 15 actions have now been completed. All the different outputs, including those delivered in an interim form in 2014, have been consolidated into a comprehensive package. The BEPS package of measures represents the first substantial renovation of the international tax rules in almost a century. Once the new measures become applicable, it is expected that profits will be reported where the economic activities that generate them are carried out and where value is created. BEPS planning strategies that rely on outdated rules or on poorly co-ordinated domestic measures will be rendered ineffective.

Implementation therefore becomes key at this stage. The BEPS package is designed to be implemented via changes in domestic law and practices, and via treaty provisions, with negotiations for a multilateral instrument under way and expected to be finalised in 2016. OECD and G20 countries have also agreed to continue to work together to ensure a consistent and co-ordinated implementation of the BEPS recommendations. Globalisation requires that global solutions and a global dialogue be established which go beyond OECD and G20 countries. To further this objective, in 2016 OECD and G20 countries will conceive an inclusive framework for monitoring, with all interested countries participating on an equal footing.

A better understanding of how the BEPS recommendations are implemented in practice could reduce misunderstandings and disputes between governments. Greater focus on implementation and tax administration should therefore be mutually beneficial to governments and business. Proposed improvements to data and analysis will help support ongoing evaluation of the quantitative impact of BEPS, as well as evaluating the impact of the countermeasures developed under the BEPS Project.

Table of contents

Abbreviations and acronyms

APA	Advance pricing arrangement
BEPS	Base erosion and profit shifting
FTA	Forum on Tax Administration
MAP	Mutual agreement procedure
OECD	Organisation for Economic Co-operation and Development

Executive summary

Eliminating opportunities for cross-border tax avoidance and evasion and the effective and efficient prevention of double taxation are critical to building an international tax system that supports economic growth and a resilient global economy. Countries agree that the introduction of the measures developed to address base erosion and profit shifting pursuant to the *Action Plan on Base Erosion and Profit Shifting* (BEPS Action Plan, OECD, 2013) should not lead to unnecessary uncertainty for compliant taxpayers and to unintended double taxation. Improving dispute resolution mechanisms is therefore an integral component of the work on BEPS issues.

Article 25 of the OECD Model Tax Convention (OECD, 2014) provides a mechanism, independent from the ordinary legal remedies available under domestic law, through which the competent authorities of the Contracting States may resolve differences or difficulties regarding the interpretation or application of the Convention on a mutually-agreed basis. This mechanism – the mutual agreement procedure (MAP) – is of fundamental importance to the proper application and interpretation of tax treaties, notably to ensure that taxpayers entitled to the benefits of the treaty are not subject to taxation by either of the Contracting States which is not in accordance with the terms of the treaty.

The measures developed under Action 14 of the BEPS Action Plan aim to strengthen the effectiveness and efficiency of the MAP process. They aim to minimise the risks of uncertainty and unintended double taxation by ensuring the consistent and proper implementation of tax treaties, including the effective and timely resolution of disputes regarding their interpretation or application through the mutual agreement procedure. These measures are underpinned by a strong political commitment to the effective and timely resolution of disputes through the mutual agreement procedure and to further progress to rapidly resolve disputes.

Through the adoption of this Report, countries have agreed to important changes in their approach to dispute resolution, in particular by having developed a minimum standard with respect to the resolution of treaty-related disputes, committed to its rapid implementation and agreed to ensure its effective implementation through the establishment of a robust peer-based monitoring mechanism that will report regularly through the Committee on Fiscal Affairs to the G20. The minimum standard will:

- Ensure that treaty obligations related to the mutual agreement procedure are fully implemented in good faith and that MAP cases are resolved in a timely manner;
- Ensure the implementation of administrative processes that promote the prevention and timely resolution of treaty-related disputes; and
- Ensure that taxpayers can access the MAP when eligible.

The minimum standard is complemented by a set of best practices. The monitoring of the implementation of the minimum standard will be carried out pursuant to detailed terms of reference and an assessment methodology to be developed in the context of the OECD/G20 BEPS Project in 2016.

In addition to the commitment to implement the minimum standard by all countries adhering to the outcomes of the BEPS Project, the following countries have declared their commitment to provide for mandatory binding MAP arbitration in their bilateral tax treaties as a mechanism to guarantee that treaty-related disputes will be resolved within a specified timeframe: Australia, Austria, Belgium, Canada, France, Germany, Ireland, Italy, Japan, Luxembourg, the Netherlands, New Zealand, Norway, Poland, Slovenia, Spain, Sweden, Switzerland, the United Kingdom and the United States.[1] This represents a major step forward as together these countries were involved in more than 90 percent of outstanding MAP cases at the end of 2013, as reported to the OECD.[2]

Notes

1. The Leaders' Declaration issued following the 7-8 June 2015 G7 Summit (available at www.g7germany.de/Content/DE/_Anlagen/G8_G20/2015-06-08-g7-abschluss-eng.pdf?__blob=publicationFile) contained the following statement regarding MAP arbitration:

   Moreover, we will strive to improve existing international information networks and cross-border cooperation on tax matters, including through a commitment to establish binding mandatory arbitration in order to ensure that the risk of double taxation does not act as a barrier to cross-border trade and investment. We support work done on binding arbitration as part of the BEPS project and we encourage others to join us in this important endeavour.

2. See www.oecd.org/ctp/dispute/map-statistics-2013.htm.

Introduction

1. At the request of the G20, the OECD published its *Action Plan on Base Erosion and Profit Shifting* (BEPS Action Plan, OECD, 2013) in July 2013. The BEPS Action Plan includes 15 actions to address BEPS in a comprehensive manner and sets deadlines to implement these actions.

2. The BEPS Action Plan recognises that the actions to counter BEPS must be complemented with actions that ensure certainty and predictability for business. The work on Action 14, which seeks to improve the effectiveness of the mutual agreement procedure (MAP) in resolving treaty-related disputes, is thus an integral component of the work on BEPS issues and reflects the comprehensive and holistic approach of the BEPS Action Plan. The relevant part of the Action Plan reads as follows:

> **The actions to counter BEPS must be complemented with actions that ensure certainty and predictability for business.** Work to improve the effectiveness of the mutual agreement procedure (MAP) will be an important complement to the work on BEPS issues. The interpretation and application of novel rules resulting from the work described above could introduce elements of uncertainty that should be minimised as much as possible. Work will therefore be undertaken in order to examine and address obstacles that prevent countries from [re]solving treaty-related disputes under the MAP. Consideration will also be given to supplementing the existing MAP provisions in tax treaties with a mandatory and binding arbitration provision.
>
> ***ACTION 14***
> ***Make dispute resolution mechanisms more effective***
>
> *Develop solutions to address obstacles that prevent countries from [re]solving treaty-related disputes under MAP, including the absence of arbitration provisions in most treaties and the fact that access to MAP and arbitration may be denied in certain cases.*

3. This Report is the result of the work carried out on Action 14. The Report reflects a commitment by countries to implement a minimum standard on dispute resolution, consisting of specific measures to remove obstacles to an effective and efficient mutual agreement procedure. The Report also reflects agreement by countries to establish a monitoring mechanism to ensure that the commitments contained in the minimum standard are effectively satisfied. The minimum standard, complementary best practices and resulting changes to the OECD Model Tax Convention (OECD, 2014) are set out in detail in Sections I.A and I.B of this Report. The framework for a peer-based monitoring mechanism is set out in Section I.C of this Report.

4. The minimum standard is constituted by specific measures that countries will take to ensure that they resolve treaty-related disputes in a timely, effective and efficient

manner. The elements of the minimum standard are set out below in relation to the following three general objectives:

- Countries should ensure that treaty obligations related to the mutual agreement procedure are fully implemented in good faith and that MAP cases are resolved in a timely manner;
- Countries should ensure that administrative processes promote the prevention and timely resolution of treaty-related disputes; and
- Countries should ensure that taxpayers that meet the requirements of paragraph 1 of Article 25 can access the mutual agreement procedure.

5. The specific measures that are part of the minimum standard are accompanied by explanations and, in some cases, changes to the OECD Model Tax Convention (changes to the existing text of the OECD Model Tax Convention appear in ***bold italics*** for additions and ~~strikethrough~~ for deletions). Other changes to the Commentary of the OECD Model Tax Convention (hereafter the "Commentary") will be drafted as part of the next update to the OECD Model Tax Convention in order to reflect the conclusions of this Report.

6. The elements of the minimum standard (which are included in boxes in this Report) have been formulated to reflect clear, objective criteria that will be susceptible to assessment and review in the monitoring process. As indicated in Section I.C, future work to develop the monitoring mechanism will include elaboration of (*i*) the Terms of Reference that will be used by peers to evaluate implementation of the minimum standard and (*ii*) the Assessment Methodology that will be used for the purposes of such monitoring.

7. The conclusions of the work on Action 14 also reflect the agreement that certain responses to the obstacles that prevent the resolution of treaty-related disputes through the mutual agreement procedure are more appropriately presented as best practices, in general because, unlike the elements of the minimum standard, these best practices have a subjective or qualitative character that could not readily be monitored or evaluated or because not all OECD and G20 countries are willing to commit to them at this stage. These best practices are therefore not part of the minimum standard. The best practices are accompanied by explanations and, in some cases, changes to the OECD Model Tax Convention.

8. Finally, the agreement to a minimum standard that will make tax treaty dispute resolution mechanisms more effective is complemented by the commitment, by a number of countries, to adopt mandatory binding arbitration. Whilst there is currently no consensus among all OECD and G20 countries on the adoption of mandatory binding arbitration as a mechanism to ensure the timely resolution of MAP cases, a significant group of countries has committed to adopt and implement mandatory binding arbitration. This commitment to MAP arbitration is set out in Section II of this Report.

I. Minimum standard, best practices and monitoring process

A. Elements of a minimum standard to ensure the timely, effective and efficient resolution of treaty-related disputes

1. Countries should ensure that treaty obligations related to the mutual agreement procedure are fully implemented in good faith and that MAP cases are resolved in a timely manner

9. The dispute resolution mechanism provided by Article 25 (Mutual Agreement Procedure) of the OECD Model Tax Convention (OECD, 2014) forms an integral and essential part of the obligations assumed by a Contracting State in entering in to a tax treaty; the provisions of Article 25 must be fully implemented in good faith, in accordance with their terms and in the light of the object and purpose of tax treaties. The elements of the minimum standard set out in Section I.A.1 are intended to ensure the full implementation of treaty obligations related to the mutual agreement procedure and the timely resolution of MAP cases.

1.1 Countries should include paragraphs 1 through 3 of Article 25 in their tax treaties, as interpreted in the Commentary and subject to the variations in these paragraphs provided for under elements 3.1 and 3.3 of the minimum standard; they should provide access to MAP in transfer pricing cases and should implement the resulting mutual agreements (e.g. by making appropriate adjustments to the tax assessed).

10. Paragraphs 1 through 3 of Article 25 provide a mechanism, independent from the ordinary legal remedies available under domestic law, through which the competent authorities of the Contracting States may resolve differences or difficulties regarding the interpretation or application of the Convention on a mutually-agreed basis. This mechanism – the mutual agreement procedure – is of fundamental importance to the proper application and interpretation of the Convention, notably to ensure that taxpayers entitled to the benefits of the Convention are not subject to taxation by either of the Contracting States which is not in accordance with the terms of the Convention. Countries should accordingly include in all of their tax treaties paragraphs 1 through 3 of Article 25, as interpreted in the Commentary (in particular paragraph 55 of the Commentary on Article 25, which refers to the situation of States whose domestic law prevent the Convention from being complemented on points which are not explicitly or at least implicitly dealt with in the Convention) and subject to the variations in these paragraphs provided for under elements 3.1 and 3.3 of the minimum standard.

11. In general, the economic double taxation that may result from the inclusion of profits of associated enterprises under paragraph 1 of Article 9 (Associated Enterprises) is not in accordance with the object and purpose of the Convention to eliminate double

taxation. In particular, the failure to grant MAP access with respect to a treaty partner's transfer pricing adjustments, with a view to eliminating the economic double taxation that may follow from such an adjustment, will likely frustrate a primary objective of tax treaties. Countries should thus provide access to MAP in transfer pricing cases. Where, in particular, treaty provisions such as paragraph 2 of Article 9 or, in the absence of paragraph 2 of Article 9, provisions of domestic law enable Contracting States to provide for a corresponding adjustment and it is necessary for the competent authorities of the Contracting States to consult to determine the appropriate amount of that corresponding adjustment with the aim of avoiding double taxation, countries should provide access to MAP. Countries should also implement any mutual agreement resulting from these and other MAP cases.

12. It is intended to make amendments to the Commentary on Article 25 of the OECD Model Tax Convention as part of the next update of the OECD Model Tax Convention in order to clarify the treaty obligation to undertake to resolve by mutual agreement cases of taxation not in accordance with the Convention.

1.2 Countries should provide MAP access in cases in which there is a disagreement between the taxpayer and the tax authorities making the adjustment as to whether the conditions for the application of a treaty anti-abuse provision have been met or as to whether the application of a domestic law anti-abuse provision is in conflict with the provisions of a treaty.

13. As provided in paragraph 26 of the Commentary on Article 25, in the absence of a special provision, there is no general rule denying MAP access in cases of perceived abuse. Paragraphs 9.1 to 9.5 of the Commentary on Article 1 are also relevant to the question of whether there is an obligation to provide MAP access in cases of abuse; paragraph 9.5 provides in particular that treaty benefits may be denied through the application of an anti-abuse provision where obtaining a more favourable treatment based on the applicable treaty would be contrary to the object and purpose of the relevant treaty provisions. The guiding principle in paragraph 9.5 will be incorporated into tax treaties through the general anti-abuse rule based on the principal purposes of transactions or arrangements (the principal purposes test or "PPT" rule) developed in the work on Action 6 of the BEPS Action Plan, according to which the benefits of a tax treaty should not be available where one of the principal purposes of arrangements or transactions is to secure a benefit under a tax treaty and obtaining that benefit in these circumstances would be contrary to the object and purpose of the relevant provisions of the tax treaty. The interpretation and/or application of that rule would clearly fall within the scope of the MAP.

14. In this regard, it should be emphasised that the obligation to provide access to the mutual agreement procedure pursuant to paragraph 1 of Article 25 is distinct from the obligation to endeavour to resolve the case pursuant to paragraph 2 of Article 25 and from any obligation to submit an issue to arbitration that may arise under treaties that contain an arbitration provision. The provisions of paragraph 1 give the taxpayer concerned the right to present a case to the competent authority where the taxpayer considers that there is or will be taxation not in accordance with the provisions of the Convention. To be admissible, a case presented under paragraph 1 must be presented within three years from the first notification of the action which gives rise to taxation not in accordance with the Convention. Once a case that meets the requirements of paragraph 1 has been accepted,

the competent authority to which the case was presented must determine whether the taxpayer's objection appears to be justified. If that is the case, that competent authority may be able to resolve the case unilaterally, *e.g.* where the taxation contrary to the provisions of the Convention is due in whole or in part to a measure taken in the State to which the taxpayer has presented its MAP case. A MAP case that has been accepted will only move to the second, bilateral stage of the mutual agreement procedure where it meets the two requirements provided by paragraph 2 of Article 25: (*i*) the taxpayer's objection appears to be justified to the competent authority to which it has been presented and (*ii*) that competent authority is not itself able to arrive at a satisfactory unilateral solution. Finally, arbitration will only be available if the relevant treaty allows arbitration of the issue that the two competent authorities are subsequently unable to resolve under the bilateral stage of the procedure paragraph 2 of Article 25.

15. With regard to the threshold issue of the acceptance of a MAP case for consideration (*i.e.* MAP access), where there is a disagreement between the taxpayer and the competent authority to which its MAP case is presented as to whether the conditions for the application of a treaty anti-abuse rule (*e.g.* a treaty-based rule such as the PPT rule) have been met or whether the application of a domestic anti-abuse rule conflicts with the provisions of a treaty, taxpayers should be provided access to the mutual agreement procedure where they meet the requirements of paragraph 1 of Article 25. If a country would seek to limit or deny MAP access in all or certain of these cases, it should specifically and expressly agree on such limitations with its treaty partners, which should include a requirement to notify treaty partner competent authorities about such cases and the facts and circumstances involved.

16. The commitment under 1.2 of the minimum standard deals only with access to MAP, which, as explained in paragraph 14, is distinct from any obligation to endeavour to resolve the case pursuant to paragraph 2 of Article 25 and from any obligation to submit an issue to arbitration that may arise under treaties that contain an arbitration provision, whether mandatory or not. That commitment should therefore not be interpreted as including any implicit commitment with respect to these other obligations. Also, States whose practices may not currently conform to that element of the minimum standard agree to make that commitment with respect to new MAP requests.

17. It is intended to make amendments to the Commentary on Article 25 as part of the next update of the OECD Model Tax Convention in order to clarify the circumstances in which a Contracting State may deny access to the mutual agreement procedure.

1.3 Countries should commit to a timely resolution of MAP cases: Countries commit to seek to resolve MAP cases within an average timeframe of 24 months. Countries' progress toward meeting that target will be periodically reviewed on the basis of the statistics prepared in accordance with the agreed reporting framework referred to in element 1.5.

18. Whilst the time taken to resolve a MAP case may vary according to its complexity, most competent authorities endeavour to reach bilateral agreement for the resolution of a MAP case within 24 months. Countries should thus commit to seek to resolve MAP cases within an average timeframe of 24 months. Countries' progress toward meeting that target will be periodically reviewed on the basis of the statistics prepared in accordance with the agreed reporting framework referred to below in element 1.5. This reporting framework will include agreed milestones for the initiation and

conclusion/closing of a MAP case, as well as for other relevant stages of the MAP process. It is also contemplated that the work to develop the reporting framework will seek to establish agreed target timeframes for these different stages of the MAP process.

1.4 Countries should enhance their competent authority relationships and work collectively to improve the effectiveness of the MAP by becoming members of the Forum on Tax Administration MAP Forum (FTA MAP Forum).

19. The Forum on Tax Administration (FTA) is a subsidiary body of the OECD Committee on Fiscal Affairs and brings together Commissioners from 46 countries[1] to develop on an equal footing a global response to tax administration issues in a collaborative fashion. The Forum on Tax Administration MAP Forum (FTA MAP Forum) is a forum of FTA participant country competent authorities created to deliberate on general matters affecting all participants' MAP programmes that has developed a multilateral strategic plan[2] to collectively improve the effectiveness of the mutual agreement procedure in order to meet the needs of both governments and taxpayers and so assure the critical role of the MAP in the global tax environment. In light of the objectives of the FTA MAP Forum – and, in particular, in view of the role of the FTA MAP Forum in monitoring the implementation of the minimum standard set out in this Report (see element 1.6 below) – countries should become members of the FTA MAP Forum and participate fully in its work.

1.5 Countries should provide timely and complete reporting of MAP statistics, pursuant to an agreed reporting framework to be developed in co-ordination with the FTA MAP Forum.

20. Since 2006, the OECD has collected and published MAP statistics from OECD member countries and from non-OECD economies that agree to provide these statistics. These statistics provide transparency with respect to each reporting economies' MAP programme as well as a comprehensive picture of the overall state of the MAP in all of the economies reporting statistics. In the context of the work on Action 14, MAP statistics should be expected to provide a tangible measure to evaluate the effects of the implementation of the minimum standard set out in this Report and will be an important component of the monitoring mechanism described in Section I.C of this Report. Countries should accordingly provide a timely and complete reporting of MAP statistics, pursuant to an agreed reporting framework that will be developed in co-ordination with the FTA MAP Forum. As noted above, this reporting framework will include agreed milestones for the initiation and conclusion/closing of a MAP case, as well as for other relevant stages of the MAP process.

1.6 Countries should commit to have their compliance with the minimum standard reviewed by their peers in the context of the FTA MAP Forum.

21. As provided above in element 1.4 of the minimum standard, countries should become members of the FTA MAP Forum and participate fully in its work. Countries should further commit to have their compliance with the minimum standard reviewed by their peers (*i.e.* the other members of the FTA MAP Forum) through an agreed monitoring mechanism that will be developed in co-ordination with the FTA MAP

Forum. A framework describing the general features of the monitoring mechanism is provided in Section I.C of this Report. Such monitoring is essential to ensure the meaningful implementation of the minimum standard provided in Section I.A of this Report.

1.7 Countries should provide transparency with respect to their positions on MAP arbitration.

22. Mandatory binding MAP arbitration has been included in a number of bilateral treaties following its introduction in paragraph 5 of Article 25 of the OECD Model Tax Convention in 2008. A footnote to paragraph 5 notes that national law, policy or administrative considerations may not allow or justify this type of dispute resolution and that States should only include the provision in the Convention where they conclude that it would be appropriate to do so, based on the factors described in paragraph 65 of the Commentary on Article 25. Based on the footnote and paragraph 65 of the Commentary on Article 25, it is unnecessary for countries to enter reservations (in the case of OECD member countries[3]) or positions (in the case of non-OECD economies[4]) on the provision. As a consequence, however, there is a lack of transparency as to countries' positions with respect to MAP arbitration.

23. In order to provide transparency with respect to country positions on MAP arbitration, the footnote to paragraph 5 of Article 25 will be deleted and paragraph 65 of the Commentary on Article 25 will be appropriately amended when the OECD Model Tax Convention is next updated. Consequential changes to the Commentary on Article 25 would also be made at the same time as these amendments. These changes to the Commentary on Article 25 will include in particular suitable alternative provisions for those countries that prefer to limit the scope of MAP arbitration to an appropriately defined subset of MAP cases.

2. *Countries should ensure that administrative processes promote the prevention and timely resolution of treaty-related disputes*

24. Appropriate administrative processes and practices are important to ensure an environment in which competent authorities are able to fully and effectively carry out their mandate to take an objective view of treaty provisions and apply them in a fair and consistent manner to the facts and circumstances of each taxpayer's specific case. The elements of the minimum standard set out in Section I.A.2 are intended to address a number of different obstacles to the prevention and timely resolution of disputes through the mutual agreement procedure that are related to the internal operations of a tax administration and the competent authority function, as well as to the transparency of procedures to use the MAP and to the approaches used by competent authorities to address proactively potential disputes.

2.1 Countries should publish rules, guidelines and procedures to access and use the MAP and take appropriate measures to make such information available to taxpayers. Countries should ensure that their MAP guidance is clear and easily accessible to the public.

25. Countries should develop and publish rules, guidelines and procedures for their MAP programmes, which should include guidance on how taxpayers may make requests for competent authority assistance. Such guidance should be drafted in clear and plain language and should be readily accessible to the public (*e.g.* made available on the websites of the tax administration and/or ministry of finance). Since such information may be of particular relevance where an adjustment may potentially involve issues within the scope of a tax treaty (*e.g.* where a transfer pricing adjustment is made with respect to a controlled transaction with an associated enterprise in a treaty jurisdiction), countries should take appropriate measures to ensure that their MAP programme published guidance is available to taxpayers in such cases.

2.2 Countries should publish their country MAP profiles on a shared public platform (pursuant to an agreed template to be developed in co-ordination with the FTA MAP Forum).

26. In order to promote the transparency and dissemination of MAP programme published guidance, countries should publish their country MAP profiles on a shared public platform (*e.g.* dedicated website). For these purposes, a "country MAP profile" should be understood as a document providing competent authority contact details, links to domestic MAP guidelines and other useful country-specific information regarding the MAP process. A template for the content of the country MAP profiles will be developed in co-ordination with the FTA MAP Forum. The development of this template will take into account the need for transparency with respect to country positions in relation to the best practices contained in this Report.

2.3 Countries should ensure that the staff in charge of MAP processes have the authority to resolve MAP cases in accordance with the terms of the applicable tax treaty, in particular without being dependent on the approval or the direction of the tax administration personnel who made the adjustments at issue or being influenced by considerations of the policy that the country would like to see reflected in future amendments to the treaty.

27. Countries' internal guidance and procedures for the operation of their MAP programmes should clearly establish that their staff in charge of MAP processes have the authority to resolve MAP cases in accordance with the terms of the applicable tax treaty, based on the objective and consistent application of treaty provisions to the specific facts and circumstances of a taxpayer's case, with a view to eliminating taxation not in accordance with the treaty. Such internal guidance and procedures should, in particular, provide that the competent authority does not require the approval or direction of the tax administration personnel who made the adjustments at issue to resolve a MAP case and that, in resolving a MAP case, the competent authority should not be influenced by considerations of the policy that the country would like to see adopted and reflected in

future amendments to the treaty (or, more broadly, to the country's preferred negotiating position with respect to all of its future treaties). The commitment to ensure that the staff in charge of MAP cases have the authority to resolve MAP cases pursuant to element 2.3 of the minimum standard must be understood to include a commitment to ensure the timely implementation of the agreements that are reached by competent authorities through the MAP process.

2.4	***Countries should not use performance indicators for their competent authority functions and staff in charge of MAP processes based on the amount of sustained audit adjustments or maintaining tax revenue.***

28. Countries' internal procedures for the operation of their MAP programmes should clearly establish that the performance of their competent authority functions and staff in charge of MAP processes shall not be evaluated based on criteria such as the amount of sustained audit adjustments or the maintenance of tax revenue. These internal procedures should instead provide that competent authority functions and staff in charge of MAP processes will be evaluated based on appropriate performance indicators, which could include –

- number of MAP cases resolved;
- consistency (*i.e.* a treaty should be applied in a principled and consistent manner to MAP cases involving the same facts and similarly-situated taxpayers); and
- time taken to resolve a MAP case (recognising that the time taken to resolve a MAP case may vary according to its complexity and that matters not under the control of a competent authority may have a significant impact on the time needed to resolve a case).

2.5	***Countries should ensure that adequate resources are provided to the MAP function.***

29. Countries should ensure that adequate resources – including personnel, funding, training and other programme needs – are provided to the MAP function, in order to enable competent authorities to carry out their mandate to resolve cases of taxation not in accordance with the provisions of the Convention in a timely and effective manner.

2.6	***Countries should clarify in their MAP guidance that audit settlements between tax authorities and taxpayers do not preclude access to MAP. If countries have an administrative or statutory dispute settlement/resolution process independent from the audit and examination functions and that can only be accessed through a request by the taxpayer, countries may limit access to the MAP with respect to the matters resolved through that process. Countries should notify their treaty partners of such administrative or statutory processes and should expressly address the effects of those processes with respect to the MAP in their public guidance on such processes and in their public MAP programme guidance.***

30. Countries' MAP programme guidance should make clear that audit settlements between the tax authorities and taxpayers do not preclude access to the mutual agreement procedure.[5] In such cases, after the mutual agreement procedure has been initiated, the competent authority should independently consider whether the audit settlement would result for the taxpayer in taxation not in accordance with the provisions of the Convention, recognising the fundamental role of the competent authority in ensuring the proper application and interpretation of a country's tax treaties. Even where the competent authority would not consider the taxpayer's objection to be justified, it should provide appropriate notification of the case to the competent authority of its treaty partner. It must be understood that the question of providing access to MAP in a case in which a taxpayer has reached an audit settlement with the tax authorities is distinct from the question of whether MAP arbitration is available (where the relevant treaty contains an arbitration provision); MAP arbitration will only be available with respect to a case that has been provided access to the mutual agreement procedure where the case satisfies the requirements of paragraph 2 of Article 25 (*i.e.* the competent authority to which the case is presented considers the taxpayer's objection to be justified), as well as those of the applicable arbitration provision.

31. Where, however, a country has in place an administrative or statutory dispute settlement or resolution process independent from the audit and examination functions and that can only be accessed through a request by the taxpayer, that country may limit access to the mutual agreement procedure with respect to the matters resolved through that administrative or statutory process. This would include, for example, a settlement process that clearly provides for a voluntary request by the taxpayer for a final audit settlement and clearly ensures that this request is made to and decided upon by a body consisting of persons that have neither directly nor indirectly been involved in the audit itself and that have the authority to independently decide on the settlement in a way that ensures that the settlement is in line with the applicable legislation, including any applicable treaty. Countries should in all cases notify their treaty partners of such processes. Countries should in addition expressly address the effects of such processes with respect to the MAP in their public guidance on these processes and in their public MAP programme guidance, in order to ensure that taxpayers who choose to make use of these processes are fully informed of the consequences as far as their access to the MAP is concerned.

32. It is expected that the issue of MAP access for cases in which there has been an audit settlement will be addressed in amendments to the Commentary on Article 25 when the OECD Model Tax Convention is next updated. These amendments would address in particular the policy considerations that support the provision of MAP access in such cases, notably the double taxation that may result where a taxpayer is required to give up the right to have questions related to the interpretation and application of a treaty resolved bilaterally through the mutual agreement procedure.

2.7 Countries with bilateral advance pricing arrangement (APA) programmes should provide for the roll-back of APAs in appropriate cases, subject to the applicable time limits (such as statutes of limitation for assessment) where the relevant facts and circumstances in the earlier tax years are the same and subject to the verification of these facts and circumstances on audit.

33. Where a country has implemented a bilateral advance pricing arrangement (APA) programme (see best practice 4 below), situations may arise in which the issues resolved through an APA are relevant with respect to previous filed tax years not included within the original scope of the APA. The "roll-back" of the APA to these previous years may be helpful to prevent or resolve potential transfer pricing disputes. Countries with bilateral APA programmes should accordingly provide for the roll-back of APAs in appropriate cases where the relevant facts and circumstances in the earlier tax years are the same and subject to the verification of these facts and circumstances on audit. The roll-back of an APA will remain subject to the applicable time limits: those provided by Article 25 where a MAP request has been or will be made with respect to the earlier tax years; or those provided by the relevant domestic law (such as statutes of limitation for assessment) where no MAP request has been or will be made with respect to the earlier tax years. Downward adjustments should only be made after notification to or consultation with the other competent authority, in order to prevent an outcome that leads to non-taxation of all or part of the adjusted profits.

3. Countries should ensure that taxpayers that meet the requirements of paragraph 1 of Article 25 can access the mutual agreement procedure

34. Certain of the main obstacles to the resolution of treaty-related disputes through the mutual agreement procedure are issues regarding the extent of the treaty obligation to provide MAP access. Such issues are likely to become more significant as a result of the work on BEPS, as more stringent rules are implemented and tax administrations are required to develop both practical experience and common interpretations in relation to new tax treaty and transfer pricing rules. The elements of the minimum standard set out in Section I.A.3 are intended to ensure that taxpayers that meet the requirements of paragraph 1 of Article 25 have access to the mutual agreement procedure.

3.1 Both competent authorities should be made aware of MAP requests being submitted and should be able to give their views on whether the request is accepted or rejected. In order to achieve this, countries should either:

- ***amend paragraph 1 of Article 25 to permit a request for MAP assistance to be made to the competent authority of either Contracting State, or***
- ***where a treaty does not permit a MAP request to be made to either Contracting State, implement a bilateral notification or consultation process for cases in which the competent authority to which the MAP case was presented does not consider the taxpayer's objection to be justified (such consultation shall not be interpreted as consultation as to how to resolve the case).***

35. The competent authorities of both Contracting States should be made aware of the MAP requests that are submitted pursuant to paragraph 1 of Article 25 and have the opportunity to provide their views on whether the MAP request should be accepted or rejected and on whether the taxpayer's objection is considered to be justified. To achieve this objective, countries should take one of two alternative approaches: (*i*) amend paragraph 1 of Article 25 to permit a request for MAP assistance to be made to the competent authority of either Contracting State; or (*ii*) implement a bilateral notification or consultation process for cases with respect to which the competent authority to which the case is presented does not consider the taxpayer's objection to be justified (making clear that such notification or consultation should not be interpreted as consultation as to how to resolve the case).

36. The following changes will be made to paragraph 1 of Article 25 and the Commentary thereon to reflect these conclusions:

Replace paragraph 1 of Article 25 by the following:

> 1. Where a person considers that the actions of one or both of the Contracting States result or will result for him in taxation not in accordance with the provisions of this Convention, he may, irrespective of the remedies provided by the domestic law of those States, present his case to the competent authority of ***either***~~the~~ Contracting State ~~of which he is a resident or, if his case comes under paragraph 1 of Article 24, to that of the Contracting State of which he is a national~~. The case must be presented within three years from the first notification of the action resulting in taxation not in accordance with the provisions of the Convention.

Replace paragraph 7 of the Commentary on Article 25 by the following:

> 7. The rules laid down in paragraphs 1 and 2 provide for the elimination in a particular case of taxation which does not accord with the Convention. As is known, in such cases it is normally open to taxpayers to litigate in the tax court, either immediately or upon the dismissal of their objections by the taxation authorities. When taxation not in accordance with the Convention arises from an incorrect application of the Convention in both States, taxpayers are then obliged to litigate in each State, with all the disadvantages and uncertainties that such a situation entails. So paragraph 1 makes available to taxpayers affected, without depriving them of the ordinary legal remedies available, a procedure which is called the mutual agreement

procedure because it is aimed, in its second stage, at resolving the dispute on an agreed basis, *i.e.* by agreement between competent authorities, the first stage being conducted exclusively ***in one of the Contracting States***~~the State of residence (except where the procedure for the application of paragraph 1 of Article 24 is set in motion by the taxpayer in the State of which he is a national)~~ from the presentation of the objection up to the decision taken regarding it by the competent authority on the matter.

Replace paragraphs 16 to 19 of the Commentary on Article 25 by the following:

16. To be admissible objections presented under paragraph 1 must first meet a twofold requirement expressly formulated in that paragraph: ~~in principle,~~ they must be presented to the competent authority of ***either Contracting State***~~the taxpayer's State of residence (except where the procedure for the application of paragraph 1 of Article 24 is set in motion by the taxpayer in the State of which he is a national)~~, and they must be so presented within three years of the first notification of the action which gives rise to taxation which is not in accordance with the Convention. The Convention does not lay down any special rule as to the form of the objections. The competent authorities may prescribe special procedures which they feel to be appropriate. If no special procedure has been specified, the objections may be presented in the same way as objections regarding taxes are presented to the tax authorities of the State concerned.

17. The ~~requirement laid on~~option provided to the taxpayer to present his case to the competent authority of either Contracting~~the~~ State is intended to reinforce the general principle that access to the mutual agreement procedure should be as widely available as possible and to provide flexibility. This option is also intended to ensure that the decision as to whether a case should proceed to the second stage of the mutual agreement procedure (i.e. be discussed by the competent authorities of both Contracting States) is open to consideration by both competent authorities. Paragraph 1 permits a person to present his case to the competent authority of either Contracting State; it does not preclude a person from presenting his case to the competent authorities of both Contracting States at the same time (see paragraph 75 below). Where a person presents his case to the competent authorities of both Contracting States, he should appropriately inform both competent authorities, in order to facilitate a co-ordinated approach to the case.~~of which he is a resident (except where the procedure for the application of paragraph 1 of Article 24 is set in motion by the taxpayer in the State of which he is a national) is of general application, regardless of whether the taxation objected to has been charged in that the other State and regardless of whether it has given rise to double taxation or not. If the taxpayer should have transferred his residence to the other Contracting State subsequently to the measure or taxation objected to, he must nevertheless still present his objection to the competent authority of the State in which he was a resident during the year in respect of which such taxation has been or is going to be charged.~~

18. ~~However, in the case already alluded to where a person who is a national of one State but a resident of the other complains of having been subjected in that other State to an action or taxation which is discriminatory under paragraph 1 of Article 24, it appears more appropriate for obvious reasons to allow him, by way of exception to the general rule set forth above, to present his objection to the competent authority of the Contracting State of which he is a national. Finally, it is to the same competent authority that an objection has to be presented by a person who, while not being a~~

~~resident of a Contracting State, is a national of a Contracting State, and whose case comes under paragraph 1 of Article 24.~~

~~19.~~ On the other hand, Contracting States may~~, if they~~ consider ~~it preferable, give~~***that*** taxpayers ***should not have*** the option of presenting their cases to the competent authority of either State***, but should, in the first instance, be required to present their cases to the competent authority of the State of which they are resident. However, where a person who is a national of one State but a resident of the other complains of having been subjected in that other State to taxation (or any requirement connected therewith) which is discriminatory under paragraph 1 of Article 24, it appears more appropriate for obvious reasons to allow him, by way of exception to the alternative rule which obliges the taxpayer to present his case to the competent authority of his State of residence, to present his objection to the competent authority of the Contracting State of which he is a national. Similarly, it appears more appropriate that***~~Finally,~~ it ~~is~~***would be*** to the same competent authority that an objection ~~has to~~***should*** be presented by a person who, while not being a resident of a Contracting State, is a national of a Contracting State, and whose case comes under paragraph 1 of Article 24. ***To accommodate the alternative rule and the exception for cases coming under paragraph 1 of Article 24***, paragraph 1 would have to be modified as follows:

> 1. Where a person considers that the actions of one or both of the Contracting States result or will result for him in taxation not in accordance with the provisions of this Convention, he may, irrespective of the remedies provided by the domestic law of those States, present his case to the competent authority of ~~either~~***the*** Contracting State ***of which he is a resident or, if his case comes under paragraph 1 of Article 24, to that of the Contracting State of which he is a national***. The case must be presented within three years from the first notification of the action resulting in taxation not in accordance with the provisions of the Convention.

Contracting States that prefer this alternative rule should take appropriate measures to ensure broad access to the mutual agreement procedure and that the decision as to whether a case should proceed to the second stage of the mutual agreement procedure is appropriately considered by both competent authorities.

19. It may be noted that if the taxpayer becomes a resident of the other Contracting State subsequently to the taxation he considers not in accordance with the Convention, he must, under the alternative rule in paragraph 18 above, nevertheless still present his objection to the competent authority of the State of which he was a resident during the period in respect of which such taxation has been or will be charged.

Replace paragraphs 31 to 35 of the Commentary on Article 25 by the following:

31. In the first stage, which opens with the presentation of the taxpayer's objections, the procedure takes place exclusively at the level of dealings between him and the competent authorities of ~~his~~ ***the*** State ***to which the case was presented***~~of residence (except where the procedure for the application of paragraph 1 of Article 24 is set in motion by the taxpayer in the State of which he is a national)~~. The provisions of paragraph 1 give the taxpayer concerned the right to apply to the competent authority of ~~the~~***either*** State ~~of which he is a resident~~, whether or not he has exhausted all the remedies available to him under the domestic law of each of the two States. On the other hand, the competent authority is under an obligation to consider whether the

objection is justified and, if it appears to be justified, take action on it in one of the two forms provided for in paragraph 2.

31.1 The determination whether the objection "appears … to be justified" requires the competent authority to which the case was presented to make a preliminary assessment of the taxpayer's objection in order to determine whether the taxation in both Contracting States is consistent with the terms of the Convention. It is appropriate to consider that the objection is justified where there is, or it is reasonable to believe that there will be, in either of the Contracting States, taxation not in accordance with the Convention.

32. If the competent authority duly approached recognises that the complaint is justified and considers that the taxation complained of is due wholly or in part to a measure taken in ***that*** ~~the taxpayer's~~State ~~of residence~~, it must give the complainant satisfaction as speedily as possible by making such adjustments or allowing such reliefs as appear to be justified. In this situation, the issue can be resolved without ***moving beyond the first (unilateral) stage of***~~resort to~~ the mutual agreement procedure. On the other hand, it may be found useful to exchange views and information with the competent authority of the other Contracting State, in order, for example, to confirm a given interpretation of the Convention.

33. If, however, it appears to that competent authority that the taxation complained of is due wholly or in part to a measure taken in the other State, it will be incumbent on it, indeed, it will be its duty – as clearly appears by the terms of paragraph 2 – to set in motion the ***second (bilateral) stage of the*** mutual agreement procedure~~ proper~~. It is important that the ***competent*** authority in question carry out this duty as quickly as possible, especially in cases where the profits of associated enterprises have been adjusted as a result of transfer pricing adjustments.

34. A taxpayer is entitled to present his case under paragraph 1 to the competent authority of ***either***~~the~~ State ~~of which he is a resident~~ whether or not he may also have made a claim or commenced litigation under the domestic law of ***one (or both) of the***~~that~~ State***s***. If litigation is pending ***in the State to which the claim is presented***, the competent authority of ***that*** ~~the~~ State ~~of residence~~ should not wait for the final adjudication, but should say whether it considers the case to be eligible for the mutual agreement procedure. If it so decides, it has to determine whether it is itself able to arrive at a satisfactory solution or whether the case has to be submitted to the competent authority of the other Contracting State. An application by a taxpayer to set the mutual agreement procedure in motion should not be rejected without good reason.

35. If a claim has been finally adjudicated by a court in ***either***~~the~~ State ~~of residence~~, a taxpayer may wish even so to present or pursue a claim under the mutual agreement procedure. In some States, the competent authority may be able to arrive at a satisfactory solution which departs from the court decision. In other States, the competent authority is bound by the court decision. It may nevertheless present the case to the competent authority of the other Contracting State and ask the latter to take measures for avoiding double taxation.

3.2 *Countries' published MAP guidance should identify the specific information and documentation that a taxpayer is required to submit with a request for MAP assistance. Countries should not limit access to MAP based on the argument that insufficient information was provided if the taxpayer has provided the required information.*

37. Element 2.1 of the minimum standard provides that countries should develop and publish rules, guidelines and procedures for their MAP programmes, which should include guidance on how taxpayers may make requests for competent authority assistance. This published MAP guidance should in particular identify the specific information and documentation that a taxpayer is required to submit with a request for MAP assistance. Where a taxpayer has provided the required information and documentation consistent with such guidance, a competent authority should not deny the taxpayer MAP access based on the argument that the taxpayer has provided insufficient information. The FTA MAP Forum will develop guidance on the specific information and documentation required to be submitted with a request for MAP assistance.

3.3 *Countries should include in their tax treaties the second sentence of paragraph 2 of Article 25 ("Any agreement reached shall be implemented notwithstanding any time limits in the domestic law of the Contracting States"). Countries that cannot include the second sentence of paragraph 2 of Article 25 in their tax treaties should be willing to accept alternative treaty provisions that limit the time during which a Contracting State may make an adjustment pursuant to Article 9(1) or Article 7(2), in order to avoid late adjustments with respect to which MAP relief will not be available.*

38. The second sentence of paragraph 2 of Article 25 provides that any mutual agreement reached by the competent authorities pursuant to that paragraph "shall be implemented notwithstanding the time limits in the domestic law of the Contracting States". Paragraph 29 of the Commentary on Article 25 recognises that this sentence unequivocally states the obligation to implement such agreements and notes that impediments to implementation that exist at the time a tax treaty is entered into should generally be built into the terms of the agreement itself. Countries should accordingly include the second sentence of paragraph 2 of Article 25 in their tax treaties to ensure that domestic law time limits do not prevent the implementation of competent authority mutual agreements and thereby frustrate the objective of resolving cases of taxation not in accordance with the Convention.

39. Where a country cannot include the second sentence of paragraph 2 of Article 25 in its tax treaties (*i.e.* where a country has a reservation or position with respect to the second sentence of paragraph 2 of Article 25), it should be willing to accept the following alternative treaty provisions that limit the time during which a Contracting State may make an adjustment pursuant to Article 9(1) or Article 7(2), in order to avoid late adjustments with respect to which MAP relief will not be available. It is understood that such a country would satisfy this element of the minimum standard where these alternative treaty provisions are drafted to reflect the time limits for adjustments provided for in that country's domestic law; it is also understood that a country that prefers to

include the second sentence of paragraph 2 of Article 25 would not be obliged to accept such alternative provisions.

[In Article 7]:

A Contracting State shall make no adjustment to the profits that are attributable to a permanent establishment of an enterprise of one of the Contracting States after [bilaterally agreed period] from the end of the taxable year in which the profits would have been attributable to the permanent establishment. The provisions of this paragraph shall not apply in the case of fraud, gross negligence or wilful default.

[In Article 9]:

3. A Contracting State shall not include in the profits of an enterprise, and tax accordingly, profits that would have accrued to the enterprise but by reason of the conditions referred to in paragraph 1 have not so accrued, after [bilaterally agreed period] from the end of the taxable year in which the profits would have accrued to the enterprise. The provisions of this paragraph shall not apply in the case of fraud, gross negligence or wilful default.

40. The following changes to the Commentaries on Article 7 and Article 9 will provide the possibility of using such alternative provisions:

Replace paragraph 62 of the Commentary on Article 7 by the following:

62. Like paragraph 2 of Article 9, paragraph 3 leaves open the question whether there should be a period of time after the expiration of which a State would not be obliged to make an appropriate adjustment to the profits attributable to a permanent establishment following an upward revision of these profits in the other State. Some States consider that the commitment should be open-ended — in other words, that however many years the State making the initial adjustment has gone back, the enterprise should in equity be assured of an appropriate adjustment in the other State. Other States consider that an open-ended commitment of this sort is unreasonable as a matter of practical administration. This problem has not been dealt with in the text of either paragraph 2 of Article 9 or paragraph 3 but Contracting States are left free in bilateral conventions to include, if they wish, provisions dealing with the length of time during which a State should be obliged to make an appropriate adjustment (see on this point paragraphs 39, 40 and 41 of the Commentary on Article 25). ***Contracting States may also wish to address this issue through a provision limiting the length of time during which an adjustment may be made pursuant to paragraph 2 of Article 7; such a solution avoids the double taxation that may otherwise result where there is no adjustment in the other State pursuant to paragraph 3 of Article 7 following the first State's adjustment pursuant to paragraph 2 of Article 7. Contracting States that wish to achieve that result may agree bilaterally to add the following paragraph after paragraph 4:***

5. A Contracting State shall make no adjustment to the profits that are attributable to a permanent establishment of an enterprise of one of the Contracting States after [bilaterally agreed period] from the end of the taxable year in which the profits would have been attributable to the permanent establishment. The provisions of this paragraph shall not apply in the case of fraud, gross negligence or wilful default.

Replace paragraph 10 of the Commentary on Article 9 by the following:

10. The paragraph also leaves open the question whether there should be a period of time after the expiration of which State B would not be obliged to make an appropriate adjustment to the profits of enterprise Y following an upward revision of the profits of enterprise X in State A. Some States consider that State B's commitment should be open-ended — in other words, that however many years State A goes back to revise assessments, enterprise Y should in equity be assured of an appropriate adjustment in State B. Other States consider that an open-ended commitment of this sort is unreasonable as a matter of practical administration. In the circumstances, therefore, this problem has not been dealt with in the text of the Article; but Contracting States are left free in bilateral conventions to include, if they wish, provisions dealing with the length of time during which State B is to be under obligation to make an appropriate adjustment (see on this point paragraphs 39, 40 and 41 of the Commentary on Article 25). ***Contracting States may also wish to address this issue through a provision limiting the length of time during which a primary adjustment may be made pursuant to paragraph 1 of Article 9; such a solution avoids the economic double taxation that may otherwise result where there is no corresponding adjustment following the primary adjustment. Contracting States that wish to achieve that result may agree bilaterally to add the following paragraph after paragraph 2:***

3. A Contracting State shall not include in the profits of an enterprise, and tax accordingly, profits that would have accrued to the enterprise but by reason of the conditions referred to in paragraph 1 have not so accrued, after [bilaterally agreed period] from the end of the taxable year in which the profits would have accrued to the enterprise. The provisions of this paragraph shall not apply in the case of fraud, gross negligence or wilful default.

41. Some countries may be willing to include the second sentence of paragraph 2 of Article 25 in their tax treaties subject to agreement to limit the time during which a Contracting State may make an adjustment pursuant to Article 9(1) or Article 7(2). This reflects the view of some countries that an open-ended commitment to make a corresponding adjustment is unreasonable as a matter of practical administration, but certainty that double taxation will be relieved is appropriate if an adjustment pursuant to Article 9(1) or Article 7(2) is made within a reasonable period. It is understood that a country would meet the minimum standard where the second sentence of paragraph 2 of Article 25 is included in its tax treaties in addition to the alternative provisions to Article 7 and Article 9 set out in paragraph 39 of this Report.

B. Best practices

42. As noted above, the work mandated by Action 14 also identified a number of best practices related to the three general objectives of the minimum standard. These best practices, which are not part of the minimum standard, are set out below.

1. Countries should ensure that treaty obligations related to the mutual agreement procedure are fully implemented in good faith and that MAP cases are resolved in a timely manner

Best practice 1: Countries should include paragraph 2 of Article 9 in their tax treaties.

43. Most countries consider that the economic double taxation resulting from the inclusion of profits of associated enterprises under paragraph 1 of Article 9 is not in accordance with the object and purpose of tax treaties and falls within the scope of the mutual agreement procedure under Article 25. See generally paragraphs 10 to 12 of the Commentary on Article 25. Some countries, however, take the position that, in the absence of a treaty provision based on paragraph 2 of Article 9, they are not obliged to make corresponding adjustments or to grant access to the MAP with respect to the economic double taxation that may otherwise result from a primary transfer pricing adjustment. Such a position frustrates a primary objective of tax treaties – the elimination of double taxation – and prevents bilateral consultation to determine appropriate transfer pricing adjustments. Element 1.1 of the minimum standard will ensure that access to MAP is provided for such transfer pricing cases. However, it would be more efficient if countries would also have the possibility to provide for corresponding adjustments unilaterally in cases in which they find the objection of the taxpayer to be justified. Countries should accordingly include paragraph 2 of Article 9 in their tax treaties, with the understanding that such a change is not intended to create any negative inference with respect to treaties that do not currently contain a provision based on paragraph 2 of Article 9.

2. Countries should ensure that administrative processes promote the prevention and timely resolution of treaty-related disputes

Best practice 2: Countries should have appropriate procedures in place to publish agreements reached pursuant to the authority provided by the first sentence of paragraph 3 of Article 25 "to resolve by mutual agreement any difficulties or doubts arising as to the interpretation or application of the Convention" that affect the application of a treaty to all taxpayers or to a category of taxpayers (rather than to a specific taxpayer's MAP case) where such agreements provide guidance that would be useful to prevent future disputes and where the competent authorities agree that such publication is consistent with principles of sound tax administration.

44. The authority provided by the first sentence of paragraph 3 of Article 25 "to resolve by mutual agreement any difficulties or doubts arising as to the interpretation or application of the Convention" may be an effective tool to reinforce the consistent bilateral application of tax treaties. Competent authorities should accordingly be encouraged to make active use of that authority. Moreover, countries should have appropriate procedures in place to publish Article 25(3) mutual agreements which relate to general matters that affect the application of a treaty to all taxpayers or to a category of taxpayers (rather than to a specific taxpayer's MAP case), where these agreements provide guidance that would be useful to prevent future disputes and where the competent authorities agree that such publication is consistent with principles of sound tax administration. It should be understood that procedures for the publication of Article

25(3) mutual agreements must include appropriate provisions to protect the confidentiality of taxpayer information.

45. It is intended to make amendments to the Commentary on Articles 3 and 25 of the OECD Model Tax Convention as part of the next update of the OECD Model Tax Convention in order to clarify the legal status of a mutual agreement entered into under Article 25(3).

Best practice 3: Countries should develop the "global awareness" of the audit/examination functions involved in international matters through the delivery of the Forum on Tax Administration's "Global Awareness Training Module" to appropriate personnel.

46. The FTA MAP Forum's Strategic Plan[6] identifies a number of specific initiatives to address particular challenges faced by competent authorities with respect to resources, empowerment, relationships and posture, process improvements, relationship with the audit function, and responsibility and accountability. A country's participation in the FTA MAP Forum reflects a commitment by participating competent authorities to advance through these initiatives the goals reflected in the Strategic Plan and to be accountable for these efforts to their FTA MAP Forum colleagues.

47. The Strategic Plan notes that increasing the "global awareness" of the audit and examination functions involved in international matters is of central importance in preventing dysfunctional tax administration behaviours (*e.g.* unprincipled adjustments to non-resident companies) and avoiding the disputes that these behaviours can create. In this regard, the Strategic Plan provides: "All audit functions involved in adjusting taxpayer positions on international matters must be aware of (1) the potential for creating double taxation, (2) the impact of proposed adjustments on the tax base of one or more other jurisdictions, and (3) the processes and principles by which competing jurisdictional claims are reconciled by competent authorities." One of the several initiatives pursued by the FTA MAP Forum is thus to encourage the delivery of training on these matters, and the FTA has prepared and approved a "Global Awareness Training Module" that may be used for that purpose. Countries should seek to develop the global awareness of the audit and examination functions of their tax administrations, making appropriate use of the FTA's Global Awareness Training Module.

Best practice 4: Countries should implement bilateral APA programmes.

48. An advance pricing arrangement (APA) is an "arrangement that determines, in advance of controlled transactions, an appropriate set of criteria (*e.g.* method, comparables and appropriate adjustments thereto, critical assumptions as to future events) for the determination of the transfer pricing for those transactions over a fixed period of time". See paragraph 4.123 of the OECD Transfer Pricing Guidelines for Multinational Enterprises and Tax Administrations. APAs concluded bilaterally between treaty partner competent authorities provide an increased level of certainty in both jurisdictions, lessen the likelihood of double taxation and may proactively prevent transfer pricing disputes. Countries should accordingly seek to implement bilateral APA programmes as soon as they have the capacity to do so.

Best practice 5: Countries should implement appropriate procedures to permit, in certain cases and after an initial tax assessment, taxpayer requests for the multi-year resolution through the MAP of recurring issues with respect to filed tax years, where the relevant facts and circumstances are the same and subject to the verification of such facts and circumstances on audit. Such procedures would remain subject to the requirements of paragraph 1 of Article 25: a request to resolve an issue with respect to a particular taxable year would only be allowed where the case has been presented within three years of the first notification of the action resulting in taxation not in accordance with the Convention with respect to that taxable year.

49. In certain cases, a request for competent authority assistance in respect of a specific adjustment to income may present recurring issues which will also be relevant in previous or subsequent filed tax years. MAP procedures that allow a taxpayer also to request MAP assistance with respect to such recurring issues for these other filed tax years – generally subject to the requirement that the relevant facts and circumstances are the same and subject to the verification of such facts and circumstances – may help to avoid duplicative MAP requests and permit a more efficient use of competent authority resources. Countries should accordingly seek to implement appropriate procedures to permit, in certain cases and after an initial tax assessment, taxpayer requests for the multi-year resolution through the MAP of recurring issues with respect to filed tax years, where the relevant facts and circumstances are the same and subject to the verification of such facts and circumstances on audit. Such procedures would remain subject to the requirements of paragraph 1 of Article 25: a MAP request to resolve an issue with respect to a particular taxable year would only be allowed where the case has been presented within three years of the first notification of the action resulting in taxation not in accordance with the Convention with respect to that taxable year (*i.e.* such procedures would not allow MAP requests that would be time-barred under paragraph 1 of Article 25).

3. Countries should ensure that taxpayers that meet the requirements of paragraph 1 of Article 25 can access the mutual agreement procedure

Best practice 6: Countries should take appropriate measures to provide for a suspension of collections procedures during the period a MAP case is pending. Such a suspension of collections should be available, at a minimum, under the same conditions as apply to a person pursuing a domestic administrative or judicial remedy.

50. Where the payment of tax is a requirement for MAP access, the taxpayer concerned may face significant financial difficulties: if both Contracting States collect the disputed taxes, double taxation will in fact occur and the resulting cash flow problems may have a substantial impact on a taxpayer's business, at least for as long as it takes to resolve the MAP case. A competent authority may also find it more difficult to enter into good faith MAP discussions when it considers that it may likely have to refund taxes already collected. Countries should accordingly take appropriate measures to provide for a suspension of collections procedures during the period a MAP case is pending. Such a suspension of collections should be available, at a minimum, under the same conditions as apply to a person pursuing a domestic administrative or judicial remedy. When the OECD Model Tax Convention is next updated, it is expected that amendments related to this best practice will be made to the Commentary on Article 25, in particular to expand on existing Commentary describing the policy considerations that support a suspension of collection procedures during the period a MAP case is pending.

Best practice 7: Countries should implement appropriate administrative measures to facilitate recourse to the MAP to resolve treaty-related disputes, recognising the general principle that the choice of remedies should remain with the taxpayer.

51. The mutual agreement procedure provided for by Article 25 is available to taxpayers irrespective of the judicial and administrative remedies provided by the domestic law of the Contracting States. Because the constitutions and/or domestic law of many countries provide that no person can be deprived of the judicial remedies available under domestic law, a taxpayer's choice of recourse is generally only constrained by applicable time limits (such as those provided by a domestic law statute of limitation or by paragraph 1 of Article 25) and by the circumstance that most tax administrations will not deal with a taxpayer's case through both the MAP and a domestic court or administrative proceeding at the same time (*i.e.* one process will typically take precedence over the other). Recognising, however, that an agreement reached through the MAP will typically provide a comprehensive bilateral resolution of a case – and thereby ensure relief from double taxation – countries should implement appropriate administrative measures to facilitate recourse to the MAP to resolve treaty-related disputes whilst observing the general principle that the choice of remedies should remain with the taxpayer.

Best practice 8: Countries should include in their published MAP guidance an explanation of the relationship between the MAP and domestic law administrative and judicial remedies. Such public guidance should address, in particular, whether the competent authority considers itself to be legally bound to follow a domestic court decision in the MAP or whether the competent authority will not deviate from a domestic court decision as a matter of administrative policy or practice.

52. The complex interaction between domestic law remedies and the MAP is generally governed by a Contracting State's domestic law and/or administrative procedures (*i.e.* a tax treaty will generally not itself contain any provisions on this point) and may thus give rise to uncertainty, particularly in light of the different approaches adopted in different jurisdictions. Such uncertainty may concern, for example, the continued availability of other remedies where a taxpayer has chosen first to pursue the MAP and the extent to which a competent authority may depart from a decision by a domestic court. Countries should thus include in their published MAP guidance (see element 2.1 above) an explanation of the relationship between the MAP and domestic law administrative and judicial remedies, including guidance on the processes involved and the conditions, rules and deadlines associated with these processes. This public guidance should specifically address whether the competent authority considers itself to be legally bound to follow a domestic court decision in the MAP or whether the competent authority will not deviate from a domestic court decision as a matter of administrative policy or practice.

53. The following changes will be made to the Commentary on Article 25 in order to clarify the issue:

Replace paragraph 35 of the Commentary on Article 25 by the following:

> 35. If a claim has been finally adjudicated by a court in the State of residence, a taxpayer may wish even so to present or pursue a claim under the mutual agreement

procedure. In some States, the competent authority may be able to arrive at a satisfactory solution which departs from the court decision. In other States, the competent authority is bound by the court decision ***(i.e. it is obliged, as a matter of law, to follow the court decision) or will not depart from the court decision as a matter of administrative policy or practice***. It may nevertheless present the case to the competent authority of the other Contracting State and ask the latter to take measures for avoiding double taxation.

Replace paragraph 42 of the Commentary on Article 25 by the following:

42. The case may arise where a mutual agreement is concluded in relation to a taxpayer who has brought a suit for the same purpose in the competent court of either Contracting State and such suit is still pending. In such a case, there would be no grounds for rejecting a request by a taxpayer that he be allowed to defer acceptance of the solution agreed upon as a result of the mutual agreement procedure until the court had delivered its judgment in that suit. Also, a view that competent authorities might reasonably take is that where the taxpayer's suit is ongoing as to the particular issue upon which mutual agreement is sought by that same taxpayer, discussions of any depth at the competent authority level should await a court decision. If the taxpayer's request for a mutual agreement procedure applied to different tax years than the court action, but to essentially the same factual and legal issues, so that the court outcome would in practice be expected to affect the treatment of the taxpayer in years not specifically the subject of litigation, the position might be the same, in practice, as for the cases just mentioned. In either case, awaiting a court decision or otherwise holding a mutual agreement procedure in abeyance whilst formalised domestic recourse proceedings are underway will not infringe upon, or cause time to expire from, the two year period referred to in paragraph 5 of the Article. Of course, if competent authorities consider, in either case, that the matter might be resolved notwithstanding the domestic law proceedings (because, for example, the competent authority where the court action is taken will not be ***legally*** bound or constrained by the court decision) then the mutual agreement procedure may proceed as normal. ***A competent authority may be precluded as a matter of law from maintaining taxation where a court has decided that such taxation is not in accordance with the provisions of a tax treaty. In contrast, in some countries a competent authority would not be legally precluded from granting relief from taxation notwithstanding a court decision that such taxation was in accordance with the provisions of a tax treaty. In such a case, nothing (e.g. administrative policy or practice) should prevent the competent authorities from reaching a mutual agreement pursuant to which a Contracting State will relieve taxation considered by the competent authorities as not in accordance with the provisions of the tax treaty, and thus depart from a decision rendered by a court of that State.***

Best practice 9: Countries' published MAP guidance should provide that taxpayers will be allowed access to the MAP so that the competent authorities may resolve through consultation the double taxation that can arise in the case of bona fide taxpayer-initiated foreign adjustments – i.e. taxpayer-initiated adjustments permitted under the domestic laws of a treaty partner which allow a taxpayer under appropriate circumstances to amend a previously-filed tax return to adjust (i) the price for a transaction between associated enterprises or (ii) the profits attributable to a permanent establishment, with a view to reporting a result that is, in the view of the taxpayer, in accordance with the arm's length principle. For such purposes, a taxpayer-initiated foreign adjustment should be considered bona fide where it reflects the good faith effort of the taxpayer to report correctly the taxable income from a controlled transaction or the profits attributable to a permanent establishment and where the taxpayer has otherwise timely and properly fulfilled all of its obligations related to such taxable income or profits under the tax laws of the two Contracting States.

54. Under the laws of some States, a taxpayer may be permitted under appropriate circumstances to amend a previously filed tax return to adjust the price for a controlled transaction between associated enterprises, or to adjust the profits attributable to a permanent establishment, in order to reflect a result in accordance (in the view of the taxpayer) with the arm's length principle. Such a taxpayer-initiated adjustment may include, for example, the filing of an amended tax return to reflect an arm's length price of a controlled transaction or other taxpayer action to adjust the previously-reported attribution of profits to a permanent establishment to conform such attribution to the separate entity and arm's length principles on which Article 7 is based. In order to ensure that competent authorities may resolve through consultation the double taxation that can arise in the case of a *bona fide* taxpayer-initiated foreign adjustment – *i.e.* any action permitted under the domestic laws of a treaty partner and undertaken at the initiative of the taxpayer to adjust the previously reported results of controlled transactions, or the attribution of profits to a permanent establishment, in order to reflect an arm's length result – countries' MAP guidance should provide that taxpayers will be allowed access to the MAP with respect to such adjustments. For such purposes, a taxpayer-initiated foreign adjustment should be considered *bona fide* where it reflects the good faith effort of the taxpayer to report correctly the taxable income from a controlled transaction or the profits attributable to a permanent establishment and where the taxpayer has otherwise timely and properly fulfilled all of its obligations related to such taxable income or profits under the tax laws of the two Contracting States.

55. The following changes will be made to the Commentaries on Articles 7, 9 and 25 in order to reflect this best practice:

Add the following paragraph 59.1 to the Commentary on Article 7:

59.1 Under the domestic laws of some countries, a taxpayer may be permitted under appropriate circumstances to amend a previously-filed tax return to adjust the profits attributable to a permanent establishment in order to reflect an attribution of profits that is, in the taxpayer's opinion, in accordance with the separate entity and arm's length principles underlying Article 7. Where they are made in good faith, such adjustments may facilitate the proper attribution of profits to a permanent establishment in conformity with paragraph 2 of Article 7. However, double taxation may occur, for example, if such a taxpayer-initiated adjustment increases the profits attributed to a permanent establishment located in one Contracting State but there is no appropriate corresponding adjustment in the other Contracting State. The elimination of such double taxation is within the scope of paragraph 3. Indeed, to the extent that taxes have been levied on the increased profits in the first-mentioned State, that State may be considered to have adjusted the profits attributable to the permanent establishment, and to have taxed, profits that have been charged to tax in the other State. In these circumstances, Article 25 enables the competent authorities of the Contracting States to consult together to eliminate the double taxation; the competent authorities may accordingly, if necessary, use

the mutual agreement to determine whether the initial adjustment met the conditions of paragraph 2 and, if that is the case, to determine the amount of the appropriate adjustment to the amount of the tax charged on the profits attributable to the permanent establishment so as to relieve the double taxation.

Add the following paragraph 6.1 to the Commentary on Article 9:

6.1 Under the domestic laws of some countries, a taxpayer may be permitted under appropriate circumstances to amend a previously-filed tax return to adjust the price for a transaction between associated enterprises in order to report a price that is, in the taxpayer's opinion, an arm's length price. Where they are made in good faith, such adjustments may facilitate the reporting of taxable income by taxpayers in accordance with the arm's length principle. However, economic double taxation may occur, for example, if such a taxpayer-initiated adjustment increases the profits of an enterprise of one Contracting State but there is no appropriate corresponding adjustment to the profits of the associated enterprise in the other Contracting State. The elimination of such double taxation is within the scope of paragraph 2. Indeed, to the extent that taxes have been levied on the increased profits in the first-mentioned State, that State may be considered to have included in the profits of an enterprise of that State, and to have taxed, profits on which an enterprise of the other State has been charged to tax. In these circumstances, Article 25 enables the competent authorities of the Contracting States to consult together to eliminate the double taxation; the competent authorities may accordingly, if necessary, use the mutual agreement procedure to determine whether the initial adjustment met the conditions of paragraph 1 and, if that is the case, to determine the amount of the appropriate adjustment to the amount of the tax charged in the other State on those profits so as to relieve the double taxation.

Replace paragraph 23 of the Commentary on Article 25 by the following:

23. In self assessment cases, there will usually be some notification effecting that assessment (such as a notice of a liability or of denial or adjustment of a claim for refund), and generally the time of notification, rather than the time when the taxpayer lodges the self-assessed return, would be a starting point for the three year period to run. ***Where a taxpayer pays additional tax in connection with the filing of an amended return reflecting a bona fide taxpayer-initiated adjustment (as described in paragraph 14 above), the starting point of the three year time limit would generally be the notice of assessment or liability resulting from the amended return, rather than the time when the additional tax was paid.*** There may, however, be cases where there is no notice of a liability or the like. In such cases, the relevant time of "notification" would be the time when the taxpayer would, in the normal course of events, be regarded as having been made aware of the taxation that is in fact not in accordance with the Convention. This could, for example, be when information recording the transfer of funds is first made available to a taxpayer, such as in a bank balance or statement. The time begins to run whether or not the taxpayer actually regards the taxation, at that stage, as contrary to the Convention, provided that a reasonably prudent person in the taxpayer's position would have been able to conclude at that stage that the taxation was not in accordance with the Convention. In such cases, notification of the fact of taxation to the taxpayer is enough. Where, however, it is only the combination of the self assessment with some other circumstance that would cause a reasonably prudent person in the taxpayer's position to conclude that the taxation was contrary to the Convention (such as a judicial

decision determining the imposition of tax in a case similar to the taxpayer's to be contrary to the provisions of the Convention), the time begins to run only when the latter circumstance materialises.

Replace paragraph 14 of the Commentary on Article 25 by the following:

14. It should be noted that the mutual agreement procedure, unlike the disputed claims procedure under domestic law, can be set in motion by a taxpayer without waiting until the taxation considered by him to be "not in accordance with the Convention" has been charged against or notified to him. To be able to set the procedure in motion, he must, and it is sufficient if he does, establish that the "actions of one or both of the Contracting States" will result in such taxation, and that this taxation appears as a risk which is not merely possible but probable. Such actions mean all acts or decisions, whether of a legislative or a regulatory nature, and whether of general or individual application, having as their direct and necessary consequence the charging of tax against the complainant contrary to the provisions of the Convention. Thus, for example, if a change to a Contracting State's tax law would result in a person deriving a particular type of income being subjected to taxation not in accordance with the Convention, that person could set the mutual agreement procedure in motion as soon as the law has been amended and that person has derived the relevant income or it becomes probable that the person will derive that income. Other examples include filing a return in a self assessment system or the active examination of a specific taxpayer reporting position in the course of an audit, to the extent that either event creates the probability of taxation not in accordance with the Convention (*e.g.* where the self assessment reporting position the taxpayer is required to take under a Contracting State's domestic law would, if proposed by that State as an assessment in a non-self assessment regime, give rise to the probability of taxation not in accordance with the Convention, or where circumstances such as a Contracting State's published positions or its audit practice create a significant likelihood that the active examination of a specific reporting position such as the taxpayer's will lead to proposed assessments that would give rise to the probability of taxation not in accordance with the Convention). Another example might be a case where a Contracting State's transfer pricing law requires a taxpayer to report taxable income in an amount greater than would result from the actual prices used by the taxpayer in its transactions with a related party, in order to comply with the arm's length principle, and where there is substantial doubt whether the taxpayer's related party will be able to obtain a corresponding adjustment in the other Contracting State in the absence of a mutual agreement procedure. ***Such actions may also be understood to include the bona fide taxpayer-initiated adjustments which are authorised under the domestic laws of some countries and which permit a taxpayer, under appropriate circumstances, to amend a previously-filed tax return in order to report a price in a controlled transaction, or an attribution of profits to a permanent establishment, that is, in the taxpayer's opinion, in accordance with the arm's length principle (see paragraph 6.1 of the Commentary on Article 9 and paragraph 59.1 of the Commentary on Article 7).*** As indicated by the opening words of paragraph 1, whether or not the actions of one or both of the Contracting States will result in taxation not in accordance with the Convention must be determined from the perspective of the taxpayer. Whilst the taxpayer's belief that there will be such taxation must be reasonable and must be based on facts that can be established, the tax authorities should not refuse to consider a request under paragraph 1 merely because

they consider that it has not been proven (for example to domestic law standards of proof on the "balance of probabilities") that such taxation will occur.

Best practice 10: Countries' published MAP guidance should provide guidance on the consideration of interest and penalties in the mutual agreement procedure.

56. Issues related to competent authority consideration of interest and penalties in the context of a MAP cases are of significant importance, particularly in light of the potential for the work on BEPS to increase pressure on the mutual agreement procedure. Countries' published MAP guidance should accordingly provide guidance on the consideration of interest and penalties in the mutual agreement procedure.

57. It is intended to make amendments to the Commentary on Article 25 of the OECD Model Tax Convention as part of the next update of the OECD Model Tax Convention in order to address issues related to the consideration of interest and penalties in the mutual agreement procedure.

Best practice 11: Countries' published MAP guidance should provide guidance on multilateral MAPs and advance pricing arrangements (APAs).

58. In recent years, the substantial increase in the pace of globalisation has created unique challenges for existing tax treaty dispute resolution mechanisms. Whilst the mutual agreement procedure provided for in Article 25 of the OECD Model Tax Convention has traditionally focused on the resolution of bilateral disputes, phenomena such as the adoption of regional and global business models and the accelerated integration of national economies and markets have emphasised the need for effective mechanisms to resolve multi-jurisdictional tax disputes. Countries should accordingly develop and include in their published MAP and advance pricing arrangement programme guidance appropriate guidance on multilateral MAPs and APAs.

59. It is intended to make amendments to the Commentary on Article 25 as part of the next update of the OECD Model Tax Convention in order to address the issue of multilateral MAPs and APAs.

C. A framework for a monitoring mechanism

60. As already noted, the conclusions of the work carried out on Action 14 of the BEPS Action Plan reflect the agreement that the implementation of the minimum standard should be evaluated through a peer monitoring mechanism in order to ensure that the commitments embodied in the minimum standard are effectively satisfied. The monitoring mechanism will have the following general features:

1. All OECD and G20 countries, as well as jurisdictions that commit to the minimum standard set out in Section I.A of this Report, will undergo reviews of their implementation of the minimum standard. The reviews will evaluate the legal framework provided by a jurisdiction's tax treaties and domestic law and regulations, the jurisdiction's MAP programme guidance and the implementation of the minimum standard in practice.
2. The core output of the peer monitoring process will come in the form of a report. The report will identify and describe the strengths and any shortcomings that exist and provide recommendations as to how the shortcomings might be addressed by the reviewed jurisdiction.

3. The core documents for the peer monitoring process will be the *Terms of Reference* and the *Assessment Methodology*. The *Terms of Reference* will be based on the elements of the minimum standard set out in Section I.A of this Report and will break down these elements into specific aspects against which jurisdictions' legal frameworks, MAP programme guidance and actual implementation of the minimum standard are assessed. The *Terms of Reference* will provide a clear roadmap for the monitoring process and will thereby ensure that the assessment of all jurisdictions is consistent and complete. The *Assessment Methodology* will establish detailed procedures and guidelines for peer monitoring of OECD and G20 countries and other committed jurisdictions by the FTA MAP Forum (see element 1.6 of the minimum standard) and will include a system for assessing the implementation of the minimum standard.
4. Both the *Terms of Reference* and the *Assessment Methodology* will be developed jointly by Working Party No. 1 and the FTA MAP Forum by the end of the first quarter of 2016.
5. The peer monitoring process conducted by the FTA MAP Forum, reporting to the G20 through the OECD Committee on Fiscal Affairs, will begin in 2016, with the objective of publishing the first reports by the end of 2017.

61. A mandate for the development of the *Terms of Reference* and the *Assessment Methodology* is contained in the Annex to this Report.

Notes

1. In addition to all OECD and G20 countries, FTA participating countries/jurisdictions include Colombia, Hong Kong China, Malaysia and Singapore.
2. See www.oecd.org/site/ctpfta/map-strategic-plan.pdf.
3. See paragraph 31 of the Introduction to the OECD Model Tax Convention.
4. See paragraph 5 of the Introduction to the Non-OECD Economies' Positions on the OECD Model Tax Convention.
5. Element 2.6 of the minimum standard does not address transfer pricing safe harbours provided under a country's domestic law and no inference should accordingly be drawn with respect to such safe harbours.
6. Available at www.oecd.org/site/ctpfta/map-strategic-plan.pdf.

II. Commitment to mandatory binding MAP arbitration

62. The business community and a number of countries consider that mandatory binding arbitration is the best way of ensuring that tax treaty disputes are effectively resolved through MAP. Whilst there is no consensus among all OECD and G20 countries on the adoption of arbitration as a mechanism to ensure the resolution of MAP cases, a group of countries has committed to adopt and implement mandatory binding arbitration as a way to resolve disputes that otherwise prevent the resolution of cases through the mutual agreement procedure. The countries that have expressed interest in doing so include Australia, Austria, Belgium, Canada, France, Germany, Ireland, Italy, Japan, Luxembourg, the Netherlands, New Zealand, Norway, Poland, Slovenia, Spain, Sweden, Switzerland, the United Kingdom and the United States; this represents a major step forward as together these countries are involved in more than 90 percent of outstanding MAP cases at the end of 2013, as reported to the OECD.[1]

63. A mandatory binding MAP arbitration provision will be developed as part of the negotiation of the multilateral instrument envisaged by Action 15 the BEPS Action Plan. The countries in this group will, in particular, be required to consider how to reconcile their different views on the scope of the MAP arbitration provision. Whilst a number of the countries included in this group would prefer to have no limitations on the cases eligible for MAP arbitration, other countries would prefer that arbitration should be limited to an appropriately defined subset of MAP cases. The work of the group of committed countries on the arbitration provision will be informed by the previous work of the Focus Group on Dispute Resolution concerning issues that have prevented the adoption of MAP arbitration and options to address them.

Note

1. See www.oecd.org/ctp/dispute/map-statistics-2013.htm.

Annex A

Mandate for the development of the *terms of reference* and the *assessment methodology*

Pursuant to element 1.6 of the Action 14 minimum standard, countries commit to have their compliance with the minimum standard reviewed by their peers – *i.e.* the other members of the FTA MAP Forum (as provided in element 1.4 of the minimum standard, countries should become members of the FTA MAP Forum and participate fully in its work). This review will take place through a monitoring mechanism, the framework for which is described in Section I.C of this Report. Such monitoring is essential to ensure the meaningful implementation of the minimum standard and will be conducted pursuant to *Terms of Reference* and an *Assessment Methodology* to be developed by the OECD Committee on Fiscal Affairs through its Working Party No. 1 on Tax Conventions and Related Questions (Working Party 1) and the Forum on Tax Administration MAP Forum (the FTA MAP Forum). The mandate for the development of the *Terms of Reference* and the *Assessment Methodology* is set out below:

Preamble

Recognising that the conclusions of the work on Action 14 of the BEPS Action Plan reflect the agreement that countries should commit to a minimum standard comprising a number of specific elements that are intended to ensure that treaty-related disputes are resolved in a timely, effective and efficient manner;

Noting that the conclusions of the work on Action 14 also include agreement that the implementation of the minimum standard should be evaluated through a peer monitoring mechanism in order to ensure that the commitments embodied in the minimum standard are effectively satisfied, and that all OECD and G20 countries, as well as jurisdictions that commit to the minimum standard, will undergo reviews pursuant to that monitoring mechanism;

Considering that the peer monitoring process will require the development of *Terms of Reference* that will be used to assess the implementation of the Action 14 minimum standard and of an *Assessment Methodology* that will establish procedures and guidelines for the peer monitoring process;

The countries participating in the OECD-G20 BEPS Project have agreed that *Terms of Reference* and an *Assessment Methodology* will be developed by the OECD Committee on Fiscal Affairs, through its Working Party No. 1 on Tax Conventions and Related Questions and the Forum on Tax Administration MAP Forum (the FTA MAP Forum) pursuant to the following mandate.

A. Objective

The OECD Committee on Fiscal Affairs through its Working Party No. 1 on Tax Conventions and Related Questions and the Forum on Tax Administration MAP Forum (the FTA MAP Forum) shall develop the core documents for the monitoring of the implementation of the Action 14 minimum standard: the *Terms of Reference* and the *Assessment Methodology*. The *Terms of Reference* will be based on the elements of the minimum standard and will break down these elements into specific aspects against which jurisdictions' legal frameworks, MAP programme guidance and actual implementation of the minimum standard are assessed; they will provide a clear roadmap for the monitoring process and thereby ensure that the assessment of all jurisdictions is consistent and complete. The *Assessment Methodology* will establish detailed procedures and guidelines for the peer monitoring of OECD and G20 countries and other committed jurisdictions by the FTA MAP Forum, which will be open to all such countries participating on an equal footing and will include a system for assessing the implementation of the minimum standard.

B. Participation

The *Terms of Reference* and the *Assessment Methodology* shall be developed jointly by the OECD Committee on Fiscal Affairs, through its Working Party 1 on Tax Conventions and Related Questions, and the FTA MAP Forum, with all countries participating on an equal footing.

C. Duration and Term

The development of the *Terms of Reference* and the *Assessment Methodology* shall start no later than November 2015. Working Party 1 and the FTA MAP Forum shall aim to conclude their work on the *Terms of Reference* and the *Assessment Methodology* by the end of the first quarter of 2016.

Bibliography

OECD (2014), *Model Tax Convention on Income and on Capital: Condensed Version 2014*, OECD Publishing, Paris, http://dx.doi.org/10.1787/mtc_cond-2014-en.

OECD (2013), *Action Plan on Base Erosion and Profit Shifting*, OECD Publishing, Paris, http://dx.doi.org/10.1787/9789264202719-en.

ORGANISATION FOR ECONOMIC CO-OPERATION AND DEVELOPMENT

The OECD is a unique forum where governments work together to address the economic, social and environmental challenges of globalisation. The OECD is also at the forefront of efforts to understand and to help governments respond to new developments and concerns, such as corporate governance, the information economy and the challenges of an ageing population. The Organisation provides a setting where governments can compare policy experiences, seek answers to common problems, identify good practice and work to co-ordinate domestic and international policies.

The OECD member countries are: Australia, Austria, Belgium, Canada, Chile, the Czech Republic, Denmark, Estonia, Finland, France, Germany, Greece, Hungary, Iceland, Ireland, Israel, Italy, Japan, Korea, Luxembourg, Mexico, the Netherlands, New Zealand, Norway, Poland, Portugal, the Slovak Republic, Slovenia, Spain, Sweden, Switzerland, Turkey, the United Kingdom and the United States. The European Union takes part in the work of the OECD.

OECD Publishing disseminates widely the results of the Organisation's statistics gathering and research on economic, social and environmental issues, as well as the conventions, guidelines and standards agreed by its members.

OECD PUBLISHING, 2, rue André-Pascal, 75775 PARIS CEDEX 16
(23 2015 39 1 P) ISBN 978-92-64-24158-9 – 2015

www.ingramcontent.com/pod-product-compliance
Lightning Source LLC
LaVergne TN
LVHW081424110826
845149LV00010B/1863

* 9 7 8 9 2 6 4 2 4 1 5 8 9 *